T0268845

Pastoral Care to the Aged

A Handbook for Lay Visitors

Neville A. Kirkwood

morehouse

HARRISBURG • LONDON

Copyright © 2005 by Neville A. Kirkwood

All rights reserved. No part of this book may be reproduced, stored in a retrieval system, or transmitted in any form or by any means, electronic, mechanical, including photocopying, recording, or otherwise, without the written permission of the publisher.

Unless otherwise noted, all scriptural quotations in this book are from the Good News Bible. Copyright © 1979 by the American Bible Society. Used by permission. All rights reserved.

Morehouse Publishing, P.O. Box 1321, Harrisburg, PA 17105
Morehouse Publishing, The Tower Building, 11 York Road,
London SE1 7NX
Morehouse Publishing is a Continuum imprint.

Cover design by Dana Jackson

Library of Congress Cataloging-in-Publication Data

Kirkwood, Neville A.
     Pastoral care to the aged : a handbook for visitors / Neville A. Kirkwood.
          p.   cm.
     ISBN 0-8192-2213-5 (pbk.)
     1. Church work with older people. I. Title.
BV4435.K58   2005
259'.3—dc22

2005003490

Printed in the United States of America

01 02 03 04 05 06 07 08 09   10 9 8 7 6 5 4 3 2 1

✦ CONTENTS ✦

*Dedicated to my late parents
Rose Alice and Harold Roy Kirkwood,
whose lives were the inspiration
that influenced my ministry.*

✦ INTRODUCTION ✦

Thirty years ago, after seventeen years in ministry in India, I returned home to Australia to take up pastoral ministry. Two elderly members of my church were in a nursing home on the other side of town. I made it a practice to visit them at least once a month. Because of transportation problems, other parishioners found it difficult to visit these elderly people, so apart from my visits, they seldom had any other pastoral fellowship from their home church. I felt sad for them, although my concern was relieved when I learned that parishioners from the church down the street from their retirement village often visited them.

Many senior citizens move into continuous care retirement communities that provide a progression from independent homes to assisted living to full-time nursing-home care. Though these communities are wonderful ways of meeting the changing needs of senior citizens, they often place residents at a distance from relatives, friends and church fellowship. Listed as "absent members" in the church directory, in the life of the parish they're often all but forgotten.

Soon after their move, many seniors may become discontent and rueful that they made the change. Others who, for one reason or another, are unable to enter into the life of the retirement village may become lonely, forlorn and almost reclusive. For some, this situation sets the stage for their minds to stagnate, stimulating the onset of dementia.

Other senior citizens are determined to end their days in their own homes. Their spouse dies and their children are leading busy lives in other neighborhoods, towns or states. So, except for telephone contact and the occasional visit, they have little physical and visual contact with those who are most important to them.

And meantime, their neighborhoods are being completely transformed as longtime residents move away or die. The familiar faces and the neighborly touch are almost lost. New neighbors, too busy with their lives and work commitments, leave no time for neighborly chats; the family that lives right next door may be virtual strangers.

Cities, towns and rural areas are filled with senior citizens who are leading unstimulating lives. Their knowledge of the world and community comes only through television and newspapers and their weekly visits to the supermarket. Some have given up going to church because many parishes, with their emphasis on growing and attracting young families, are uninterested in the older folk. Even fewer parishioners seem to have the desire to listen to and hold a conversation with their more senior members. As longevity increases, more and more seniors are trapped in these situations—and for longer periods. The challenge to the modern church is to become actively aware of the aged in their community who need pastoral interest and care—whether they're in nursing homes, retirement communities or their own homes.

This is a critical challenge, and it won't go away. The average life expectancy is rising fast, as it becomes more common for people to live into their nineties and even beyond a hundred years. Increased life expectancy is heightening the previously recognized physical, social and economic problems the elderly face. The importance of this challenge may be perceived by looking at the statistics and projections on aging for both the United States and Australia.

In the U.S. Census in 2000, there were 35 million people 65 years of age and older. This is an increase of 12 percent.[1] In 2003, the data indicated an additional 900,000 people in this age bracket. By 2030, projections show there will be 71.5 million people 65 years and older; this is double the number of the 2000 census. The U.S. Census estimate for 2050 rises to 86.8 million.[2]

In Australia, with a total population of 20 million, those in the over-65 age bracket in 2002 numbered 2.5 million. The following are future projections: 2012—3.1 million; 2022—4.5 million; 2032—5.5 million; 2042—6.2 million. The forecast is that by 2050 there will be as many people over the age of 50 as under that age. Another interesting statistic is that the proportion of the Australian population over the age of 65 years in 1870 was 2 percent, which contrasts with the 12 percent in 1998.[3]

1. U.S. Census Bureau, "The 65 years and over population: 2000." (October 2001): 1.

2. U.S. Administration on Aging, based on estimates of the U.S. Census Bureau. Updated November 2004.

3. Talina Drabsch, "Aging in Australia," A New South Government Briefing paper (September 2004): 1.

This situation is exacerbated by the decline of the extended family's age-old cultural responsibility of providing a lifetime of support to its members. The struggle for survival is now concentrated on members of the younger nuclear family. Society now expects the government and other social agencies to accept responsibility for the aged and their problems, making retirement homes and government agencies indispensable for many of the aged in our industrialized societies.

The church, by recognizing the needs of the elderly, is one of the agencies taking up some of the slack that budget deficits have forced governments to leave. Churches are playing a small part in meeting the physical, social and economic needs of the elderly. Churches have a significant role in some countries, with the establishment of retirement villages and nursing homes, and in some cases churches are the pioneers in this area. They provide transport to take their aged to fulfill medical or other appointments and church activities. In churches where the older membership is high, special programs have been initiated to cater to the interests of the elderly. Other churches organize concert parties and other entertainment at the church or in the retirement villages. Activities such as mornings together over coffee for socializing and indoor craft activities for keeping minds alert and fingers supple are organized. Churches may be involved in organizing or providing workers for the "Meals on Wheels" program for the less mobile. Though they've made some strides in providing for the physical needs of the elderly, churches need to do more to meet their spiritual needs. The chaplain in retirement villages fortunate enough to have one has so many to care for that she or he may not be able to bring news and comfort from a resident's home church. Very few churches find ways for members to care for the pastoral needs of the elderly parishioners.

This kind of lay pastoral care is necessary because so many who are unable to get out to participate in many of the church activities long for some fellowship from the church apart from being taken to and from the Sunday service. An increasing sense of uselessness lowers the self-esteem of these elderly parishioners. Many of these once-active and capable people feel they are on the scrap heap. Believing they are of no earthly use, they fall into depression—sometimes a deep clinical depression—and experience negativity about life generally. This mental attitude makes them all the more susceptible to psychological and physical illness, creating an even greater burden to carry.

Pastoral care and lay pastoral visitation from the church to our senior citizens are both positive ways of helping to raise the self-esteem of the aged and lifting their negativity and depression. The regular visits of a sincerely interested visitor rebuild the confidence and deepen the spiritual awareness of a joyless senior who now feels valued and recognized by society. In some cases, effective pastoral visitation can reincorporate the despondent older person back into social activity in the community, the institution and the life of the church.

This book is an effort to encourage lay members of the church to join the rewarding ministry of becoming pastorally responsible for older members of their congregation—and their community.

→ ONE ←

Understanding
the Aging Process

The big "6 0" may be a major milestone in a person's life. It comes with a warning of the closing of the middle years, as retirement stares the birthday woman or man in the face. Before the end of the next decade, they'll be collecting Social Security or the Aged Pension and people will be starting to consider them "seniors"—a polite way of saying that they're getting on in years and now may be considered among the elderly citizens. Why are the sixties the years when people begin to feel that life is passing them by? In the fifties, old age seemed millennia away. It was hardly thought about. The possible exception is the thought of anticipating getting their hands on their superannuation or retirement fund and living it up. Many do this by taking overseas trips, buying new property, refurbishing and making other expensive purchases. But the picture of the sixties begins to take on a more somber hue. Minds and bodies are beginning to tell the aging that they are not as spry as they used to be; the age of decline has begun. Remember that there are wide variations between what some see as the ravages of time and what others, plunging into new and selected interests, see as a graceful movement into further productive, fulfilling years. Everybody ages differently.

Aging is a natural function of the human body. The body, a marvelous, complex combination of living cells that interact to enable the animation of all the parts of the body, functions as a whole. During the course of the life of these cells, the body divides them a set number of times, then replaces them with new cells. However, with the passing of the years, there is progressive weakening and deterioration in the functioning of the various systems sustaining the life of the body. New cells aren't replaced as regularly. Where parts of the body are injured or diseased, the cell replacement often breaks down. Even normal cells begin to slow this process of division and replacement. Thus by seventy-five years of age, the average person's cell count is considerably depleted. Basically the symptoms of aging include:

- Weakened immune system, with a greater tendency to contract seasonal infections, viruses and other illnesses
- Greater likelihood of developing heart disease and cancer
- Adverse changes in body mass and muscle tone
- Failing memory, learning and ability to change and manage new situations
- Changes in the sensory organs: touch, hearing, sight, taste and smell are less acute, slower and weaker to respond and function

For many, if not for most, there is a decline in alertness and physical activity. Much of this is dependent on the nature and the tempo of the life lived in the first sixty years, as well as health factors. A creative mind full of initiative and ideas that has not been impeded by serious health problems may be able to remain keen, alert and sharp for another thirty or so years. Some people, as active at eighty as they were at fifty, may serve as pastoral visitors to the aged, bringing blessing to those many years younger than themselves!

Evidence of the Age of Decline

At work, around the home or in social activities, people may find that things seem to take longer to do, or they're not quite up to their previous standard of efficiency. In the fifties, it wasn't such an effort to be outside playing vigorously with the grandchildren. Ten years later, the story may be different. The muscles don't seem to have the same strength or flexibility. In the fifties, it was possible to still pitch a baseball with some speed, bowl a cricket ball on line and length or place a good lob on the tennis court. Ten years later, it may be getting harder and slower to get any accuracy. Now, in the seventies people may be reluctant to pick up a ball or a tennis racquet at all. Flexibility in movement seems to have taken a vacation. Even those who exercise regularly may experience respiratory distress: when shopping or lifting things from the car into the house, they may need to stop and catch their breath.

Often the capacity for hard work, the quickness of mind, the ability to see things quickly and the capacity to pick up the thread of conversations have dwindled. This decreasing adeptness at normal, everyday functions is often due to the degeneration of sight, hearing, subtlety of touch and sensitivity to smell. This deterioration occurs in most people aged sixty and over, to a greater or lesser degree. We cannot escape such eroding of our faculties. Our bodies, like all earthly things, degenerate, wear out and decay.

This often happens concurrently with what might be called the rusting of talents. Retirement in the sixties means a radical change of lifestyle. Normal daily occupations using hands, minds and even emotions to achieve efficient results are no longer under such pressure. For some, it is a movement into a more relaxed, leisurely way of living, as the old occupational skills are no longer called into use. In a paper to a conference a few years ago entitled, "After Retirement—What?" I urged conference participants to maintain some of their personal integrity by finding an outlet for the use of old skills and interests during their days of retirement.[4]

So many retirees fail to do this and as a consequence may lose interest in life generally. I believe it is for this reason that some hyperachiev-

---

4. The Annual Conference of the Australian Health and Welfare Association in Melbourne, February 1993.

ing, driven, executive types, when released from the pressures of their work, die soon after their pressure-cooker lid is lifted. It is the rusting of their talents that creates the stress, which breaks down their bodily systems. Uncharacteristic personality changes arise out of such frustration, as these people move further into retirement and lose the opportunities to use the gifts they once used daily.

The nature of the life lived in early years, the influences of childhood and their psychological impacts, inherited genetic health factors, the physical environment of the life, the nature of the marriage and other relationships, the workplace and social conditions all have a bearing on the physical, economic and mental health in later years. The ramifications of these conditions begin to show evidence of their effects prior to the sixties, but the consequences are more clearly outlined and often more rapid after retirement.

The American Psychiatric Association, in its *Diagnostic and Statistical Manual*, identifies in detail fifteen or so personality disorders that are the result of the social impact on the mind, affecting behavior, competence and judgment. Similarly, psychiatric disorders, such as bipolar disorder as well as other conditions that are caused by chemical imbalances in the brain, have repercussions throughout the whole of a person's life.[5] Poor nutrition, often caused by overindulgence in fast food and sodas, can lead to heart problems, diabetes, obesity and a host of other chronic health conditions. Behaviors such as addiction to alcohol, smoking, drugs and the sniffing of gasoline, paint or aerosol cans can impair mental function and lead to cancer and other disabilities. These all affect the rate of deterioration in the senior years, if not earlier. Cerebral palsy, multiple sclerosis, motor neuron disease and other neurological disorders and the like also have their repercussions on life in senior years.

Age brings a natural degeneration of the body as it wears out. The signs that accompany it are often the result of the type of life lived in early years. The external indicators of this are more commonly seen in the physical features of the face. The face and general condition of the person who has overindulged in alcohol clearly show the marks of such insobriety as he or she ages. The outdoor person who has been exposed to the sun and the weather bears the marks of

5. The American Psychiatric Association, *Diagnostic and Statistical Manual of Mental Health IV.* Washington, DC: American Psychiatric Publishing, 1994.

such weathering with coarser skin that's often tanned and dried.

Living in hot climates, where people flock to the beach to swim and sunbathe, can lead to skin conditions that are accentuated by the aging process. Wrinkles around the face and across the cheeks, crow's-feet around the eyes and furrows across the brow—often exacerbated by a lifetime of sun exposure—continue to be more pronounced as the years pass. The fear of this evidence of aging is keeping cosmetic companies—as well as cosmetic surgeons—in business. People as young as thirty are having facial treatment to reduce that telltale evidence. Skin, body shape, varicose veins and muscle wastage all bear witness to the passing of the years.

A degenerative condition that usually begins to manifest itself in midlife and beyond is osteoporosis, a condition that causes shrinkage of the bone as bone density decreases along with bone strength. This condition may lead directly to the fractures that many elderly people suffer.

The overwhelming majority of those who suffer from osteoporosis are women. For women the condition is caused by the reduction of the hormone estrogen after menopause. This hormone helps the bone to absorb the mineral calcium, which strengthens the bone. Causes for this above-normal reduction in estrogen have been traced to genetics, small bone structure, poor nutrition, low weight and steroid medications.

When you visit someone who suffers from osteoporosis, you may hear of multiple bone fractures, particularly of the spine, hip and wrist. You may have already noticed the loss of height and the more obvious rounding of the shoulders with a hump in the middle of the back just below the neck—sometimes called the "dowager's hump." As a pastoral visitor you may be able to identify osteoporosis, a major factor in hastening the evidence of aging. Mineral and vitamin supplements may help these patients.

There are many seniors who grow old gracefully. A mellow, understanding softness attracts both young and old alike. People seek these seniors out because it's so comfortable and rewarding to be in their company. They may continue to be involved in the community, the church or helping ministries. Aging makes them more winsome and engaging.

But others experience the opposite as they move into the senior years. In some, resentment of missed opportunities in earlier life builds bitterness toward the world generally. Retirement constantly involves changes, which are made more difficult by the physical changes of aging. Resentment grows with the further loss of regular employment, the deteriorations of health, the restrictions of mobility or the absence of many social contacts. This resentment sours the personality, which negatively affects relationships and moods and creates unnecessary stress and melancholy. Personalities may change from outgoing, warm and responsive into cold, manipulative, calculating, critical, withdrawn and self-centered. Those who dwell on the changes and the losses may begin to lose their motivation and miss the challenge that new interests, new people and different activities bring. Many are even satisfied to just sit and relax in their recliner and stare blankly as the days pass by. Attempts to converse with them often are met with terse, cryptic responses.

The age of decline is generally characterized by the loss of many things. Any loss brings with it a measure of grief. The more significant the loss, the greater the deterioration in condition. Grief may be experienced over the loss of prestige of leadership, of memory, of business and relational prowess, of loved ones and friends through death or relocation, of a pet, of home and personal possessions, of the ability to drive a car and particularly of a long-loved spouse or child. Such grief contains a sense of injustice and an unwillingness to accept such losses. And those who simply deny the loss may be living in a false world, unable to face reality. As real life becomes blurred by living in such a fantasy world, all sorts of odd behavior can be expected. A surviving spouse may take on some of the characteristics and actions of the deceased partner, trying to do the same things, using the same way of speaking, eating the same foods or even wearing her or his clothes and slippers around the house, keeping the association alive and continuing the denial.

Those seniors constantly concerned about this aging experience may develop a pessimistic, joyless view of life. Thoughts of the future hold menacing threats that are seen as omens of panic and dull, uninteresting days. This age of decline may be very positive and rewarding or it may be negative and despairing for those in their older years. The pastoral visitor, alert to and accepting of these differences, must spend time with all those he or she is expected to visit. It is often the despondent older person who needs pastoral ministry the most.

Factors Hastening Decline

We've identified much of the nature of the decline, which is more rapid for some than for others, in these senior years. Now is the time to look at some of the factors that hasten this decline.

Media

In the twenty-first century, images of beauty and outward appearances bombard us as if they are almost the most important human consideration. Advertising promotes creams and diets that promise beautiful faces and slim bodies. The propaganda shouts aloud that showing our age is a sin. In those sixty and over, most faces give evidence of passing time. The face in the mirror contradicts the images in the media and reinforces the thought that inevitably the years are speeding by and that seniors are on the slippery slide of aging. Dwelling on the subject each time the aging look at their reflected face, their minds harbor regret and they may be angry at their age. Such reactions accelerate the normal progress of aging.

Past Habits and Lifestyles

The passing of the years usually brings physical and emotional strains and stresses and hampers the ability to be physically active. Sports injuries, injuries from workplace accidents, the lack of care of the mind and body, the excesses of addictions, exposure to health hazards, and the invasion of arthritis in the joints all exacerbate the process of growing old. As the years go by, the abuses that people subjected their bodies to in the past may lead to more physical incapacities and restrictions of mobility.

Intellectual Curiosity

As people age, they tend to shift their intellectual pursuits down a gear or two until serious mental activity is at a minimum. The less reading they do—except for a light novel, a glance at the newspaper, the sports page or the comic strips—the more the mind begins to atrophy the less they desire to try new things.

Psychological Issues

The lessening of physical powers, as well as the growing sense of dependency on others to do certain things for seniors, is part of the aging cycle. There are those who become overly concerned by this cycle of decline and become fearful of what may come next. This fear may become neurotic as they magnify every little difference they see, feeling it is the beginning of the end. Throwing in the towel in this type of neurosis in the aged can bring a rapid fall into a dependency role.

Age catches up with us all the time—even those who have always enjoyed good health. The more healthy types may become agitated by the first signs of slowing down, seeing every ache and muscle twinge as an oncoming major disaster. Up to this time they have been relatively pain free, so they may have a very low pain threshold: a sprain is believed to be a broken ankle, indigestion causes a rush to doctor for a heart checkup, diarrhea is certainly the first sign of bowel cancer. This fretfulness over anticipating the worst raises the anxiety levels, sometimes providing the groundwork for the psychosomatic development of the illnesses that they fear.

All are aware that as the senior years come, senior moments occur when a name, an appointment time, a phone number and so on drop out of the mind's computer, to be recovered when the pressure to remember is eased. Some see this as a matter of shame and disgrace, a signal to the world that the brain is dying and soon they'll be in psychiatric care. Others may see it as the onset of Alzheimer's disease and set worry's panic button into overdrive as they foresee a downward spiral of mental deterioration. By reacting in this way, their worry will develop the condition more quickly. A healthier response is to accept it as a sign of aging and continue cheerfully on in the assurance that significant loss of memory—if any—won't happen for a long time.

A person who has been a good administrator, a social leader, an innovative organizer or an honored employee is now retired with no opportunity for a replacement leadership role. In the "sea change" retirement environment where there are a number of retirees jockeying for every office in the community, they have to live without the adrenal rushes that creative leadership can bring. So they sit like a lonely cormorant on a solitary rock, immobile as they watch for any unsuspecting fish of opportunity that might swim into their waters.

This sedentary lifestyle causes them to watch the tide of life ebb and flow. A waning confidence in their ability, frustration at their restricted lifestyle and the financial inability to splurge as they used to do leaves them with a feeling of "woe is me."

Changes and Challenges of Retirement

Aging can also bring about a loss of identity. Retirement offers fewer and fewer prospects for meaningful contributions to the community, forcing a disengagement with the outside world that can begin to fill the elderly with a deep despondency. Their local church, whose leadership roles may be filled with younger persons, might consider them to be pew warmers on a Sunday, except to drive shut-ins to appointments or help with "Meals on Wheels." Being a chauffeur is not what retired life was meant to be.

These are some of the many factors that only hasten the deterioration of the aging process. A pastoral visitor needs to consider these factors during visits. Every little bit of encouragement is helpful—even suggesting some possible goals to aim for or tasks to do. A person with some musical ability might be persuaded to link up with others of similar interests to form a group or organize regular musical entertainment for those of similar age. A person with organizing skills may be able to seek out the possibility of a monthly or more frequent bus day trips to places of interest. Such trips may be able to integrate residential care and independent care seniors into broader socialization opportunities. Activities that do not cost much, such as competitions for board games, bowling, talent shows and flower shows are possibilities. Such activities must be organized by the seniors themselves to reactivate skills, restore a sense of pride and dignity to themselves, stimulate the mind and boost a sense of continuing usefulness. To prove to seniors that they don't just have to sit but may be able to spread their wings and do some flying again, a pastoral visitor may give them an incentive to move off the rock and wade in the water.

TWO

Ministering in a
Variety of Settings

Where and with whom should pastoral visits be made? When we speak of the aged, we often think of people residing in retirement villages where three forms of accommodation are provided: independent living quarters, assisted-living units with meals provided in a communal dining room, and a nursing-home section for those who require twenty-four-hour care. Retirement community and nursing home residents may be classified as being in residential care.

The majority of the elderly, however, still live in their own homes or in private homes with their relatives or a companion. These, along with the first group in the retirement village, may also be said to be living independently. That is, they

are not under institutional care and are completely independent, although some may rely on visiting nurses to supervise and provide any medical assistance, or use "Meals on Wheels." There
is another important group of the aged who may
be under institutional care or who may live in the
community with relatives or friends. They have
what we call *dementia*.

In this chapter we will explore how to visit
people who are in residential care institutions,
older persons who are living independently, and
those who suffer from dementia, whatever their
living arrangements. Each of these groups of elderly people live under different circumstances
and have different needs that a lay pastoral visitor needs to understand before undertaking this
type of ministry.

Residential Care

Residential care is necessary when elderly people or their relatives are unable to maintain sufficient care for the needs of the aging process.
The spouse may have died and independent living becomes too traumatic, with painful memories of the loss of love and companionship
stirred wherever the person moves around the

family home. Having to cater and cook for one and to constantly eat alone creates stress at the absence of warm and happy conversation once enjoyed daily.

Residential care has many compensatory factors. It may help the resident achieve these perspectives:

- This is my new life. "We" no longer applies. This is "me" as a single person. I have to carve out a new life independent of the past. This is my present identity.
- This is my new security. All fear of living on my own is gone. If any problems should arise there are people around to help me. I am not alone. The retirement village is my new shield and protection from the traps of having to live by myself.
- This is my new source of companionship. There are enough people here to pick and choose those with whom I can develop a genuine friendship.
- This is my new sense of orderliness. The village offers organization with certain rules while providing a comfortable range of independence.
- This is my place of eased responsibilities. The burdens of home maintenance, mortgage pay-

ments or rent, household repairs, gardening and shopping are all relieved.

- This is my place of stimulation. Residential care has a recreational hall and sporting opportunities suitable for my age and fitness. There is a library. There are regular entertainments, visiting speakers, and chances to use my untapped skills such as painting, woodwork and craft making. More importantly, I have an increasing sense of enjoyment, well-being and satisfaction with life.

Much of your visitation may be to those in residential care. Although the above statements are basically true, you will soon discover that among the residents there's quite a mix of emotions. As a pastoral visitor don't assume that you'll approach every person in the same way. If you've known them in their home before their move to the village, or if you've become acquainted through the church, don't be surprised if you notice definite personality changes. Their transfer of residence will have stirred up positive and negative emotions, which we will now consider.

Positive Emotions

While living alone at home, the difficulty of maintaining a tidy home, the feeling of dependence on others to take them shopping or the need for others to do their errands for them or take them to church may have made elderly people feel useless and dependent. Entry into the village lifted a heavy weight from their mind. The move was a tremendous relief. They were not being obligated to be a recipient of charity because they were now paying for the services they received.

Living on their own meant that there were hours of loneliness and boredom. Their ability to concentrate on reading or crafts was lessening. The television was on just to hear the sound of voices, even when there was nothing worth watching. The move to the village has brought them into contact with others and provided the opportunity for meaningful conversation, which they could choose to be involved in if they felt like it.

The routine of the home seldom varied. The same visitors came and there seemed little to talk about. Now, there were new people, new activities, new learning opportunities and the constant coming and going of staff and visitors. Even those who came to visit other residents often included them in their conversations, opening their mind to new concepts and understanding of different spheres of life. Entry into the village provided new challenges to adapt to new ways and new people. It was stimulating.

Living with a relative meant the elderly persons were often left on their own. Every time the relative went out the same orders were issued: "Here's the number I'll be at—if you have a chest pain or need help just call me." "I've left a thermos of hot water on the kitchen counter—don't put the kettle on." "Don't try to walk without your walker." So it would go on. The elderly were made to feel like useless clots and imbeciles. Now, in the pleasant environment of the retirement village, they are enjoying a new freedom.

At home, they often thought about what would happen if they died in their sleep: they'd forgotten their medicine a couple of times and suffered for it. Now these worries have been eliminated and they feel secure with trained staff always available to check up on the medication.

Negative Emotions

There's a down side to every situation, of course, and life in a retirement village is no exception. Making the move into residential care means abandoning the family home and dispersing personal possessions to family and friends; even cherished furniture brought from a childhood home or the early days of a marriage may have been consigned to a thrift shop or a yard sale. Leaving so many personal things—perhaps a pet or even close neighbors and longtime friends—may fill retirement community dwellers with serious grief to face and resolve.

Anger and frustration arise at their inability to look after themselves as they once did. The move is a major eroding of their independence and dignity. This anger may be expressed at times toward the staff and even you as a visitor.

Many people look on residential care as simply the last stopping place before heaven. For some, arrival at the village heralds a warning to expect further deterioration in their ability to manage themselves and their affairs. Perhaps they envisage dementia galloping toward them like a horse, or the looming specter of life confined to a wheelchair or a recliner. A fear of the future and the possibility of serious incapacities fills them with dread as they see some residents of the nursing facility. When that sense of fear persists, depression may entrench itself in the mind.

While the loneliness of living alone is alleviated by the companionship residential care offers, negative feelings often persist because none of the people who now surround them measures up to the familiar faces and things from the past. The negative feelings engendered by the dissipation of skills, abilities, creativity and friendships, the forced inactivity, the regimentation of life in a community and the restrictions of age can make the person in residence very pessimistic, negative and sour with life. People in retirement villages may become grumpy old men and women with a constant chip on their shoulders. Don't react negatively to such whiny and complaining aged persons.

Much of the negativity of such residents may be justified. Often they're not treated as adults because there are so many who need the same intensity of care that you would give to a child. Some residents are in their second childhood and some staff may tend to treat all alike, talking down to them. Other residents have so many of their physical faculties impaired that they cannot help themselves as an ordinary adult. Much of their privacy has been stripped by staff entering their room without knocking, by being exposed during a medical examination in front of a number of staff, with the door being left open for any passersby to peer in, with total disregard for their modesty. Perhaps they've been left to public view while sitting on a commode or toilet. In their presence, staff may discus their medical problems, their treatment, even their financial situation as if they were not worthy of—or should not be involved in—the discussion. Another bone of contention may be that personal food likes and dislikes are never considered. The resident may feel like no more than a regimental number in the vast and impersonal organization.

It is inevitable that you'll hear these complaints from some of the seemingly grumpy old persons. To try to defend the institution would be another grievance to be added to the resident's already long list. If you sense the person has a genuine grievance, discuss the matter with your parish team leader so that diplomatic action may be taken at a higher level if necessary.

Any on-the-ground action you take could result in your being banned from your visitation role. You may discover by this course of action that all is not as the resident perceives or that some of the complaints may be corrected as similar situations have been reported.

Any pastoral visitor to a new resident must understand that this is a transitional period and expect a wide range of emotions, including those outlined here. Often relatives are protective of their loved ones and even feel guilty that they're not doing the caring themselves. So they may adopt a belligerent attitude toward the staff. The pastoral visitor who knows the family—particularly if they're associated with the same church— should gently inform the relatives that a wide range of reactions, many of them negative, is to be expected in the settling-in stage and even beyond.

Independent Living

Your pastoral visit to aging persons at home is quite different from visiting them in a retirement village. Unless they are under home care for serious incapacity or illness and are supported in this by family and medical home visits, the relationship will be vastly different. They may have most of their faculties, though they may not be as sprightly as they were a quarter of a century ago. They will be enjoying the freedom that independent living offers, usually surrounded by personal furniture, mementos and other cherished possessions. They will have a choice of food and will have the liberty to come and go as they please. They will be able to invite and entertain family and visitors of choice. Their dignity and self-esteem won't have been downgraded by institutionalization. With the exception of some "senior moments" of momentary memory lapses, conversations are usually possible in independent living situations. In such a home situation, your visit will generally be appreciated if you are from the same church fellowship. Such visits can be stimulating for the one you are visiting and very enriching and enjoyable for yourself. The elderly person's age may have curtailed many outdoor activities and trips; this frequently means that opportunities to socialize with others also have been reduced. Your visit is a welcome chance for a senior citizen to catch up with familiar interests.

At this time of their lives, the elderly are prone to do some reminiscing over significant events in their lives and the life of the church and its personalities. Sometimes you become a captive audience, even though you may have heard these tales before. Keep in mind that patient listening is a ministry in itself. There is no need to feel your visit was a failure because there was little talk of spiritual things. You have shown by your patient presence that the church still cares for this aged member of the fellowship. Your visit has served a useful purpose in the other's day.

In one of my parishes, every Sunday before the 11 a.m. worship service I would visit some of these mentally alert, elderly shut-ins, sharing an outline of my sermon and praying with them. These visits were no longer than twenty minutes. I'd also try to visit parishioners who were in the hospital. Most Sunday mornings, I made up to six such visits. These aged shut-ins, made to feel part of the church, had a chance to participate in some form of worship that day. As a lay pastoral visitor, your sharing of the Sunday service and its teaching—even during the week—is a wonderful piece of spiritual therapy. It gives a real sense of awareness and belonging to the fellowship, allowing parishioners to feel that they're part of the spiritual life of the church.

The person whose home you are visiting may be living alone or with a son or daughter and their family. You will obviously know whether your fellow parishioner is single or has a partner. Those who are single may have a storehouse of memories. Why are they on their own? Are they divorced or widowed, or have they remained unmarried? What are the events that led to that status? Those memories of events may harbor many sacred episodes or hurtful, destructive encounters, but uncovering those memories may heal much sorrow and regret. The reliving of past events by such narration may stir euphoria and thanksgiving, as the elderly are transported into another time and world, showering them with tranquillity and a peaceful radiance and ensuring hope for the future. The sadder moments of recall may bring resolution to some unfinished business of yesteryear that elderly people can now put behind them.

Conversely, to scratch old wounds may resurrect pain and regrets of the past, and some memories best remain interred. Be careful that you are not uncovering an unexploded bomb to blow up in both of your faces. It may scatter too much distress. As a visitor you must be continually looking for some positive aspects of the story to highlight in order to quell some of the outburst. However by this time it must be obvious that this volatile outburst should not be squashed. Any strong efforts to pour oil on the anger prematurely may result in a tirade against you and destroy any ability to be of further assistance to the person. The festering, internal boil has burst; your empathic understanding can help a transforming personality to emerge, like a butterfly emerging from the chrysalis. Such a release may have been niggling for decades and needs airing, if peaceful final years are to be enjoyed. The troubled one needs a peaceful presence, one who does more than sympathize and who is not shocked or critical at being part of this healing release. Any attempt by the visitor to take the opposite side or show abhorrence at the story may only further embitter the situation. The elderly may simply need someone to hear the depth of their hurt and bitterness before healing can commence.

As a pastoral visitor who has earned the confidence to be privy to such intimate secrets of the past, you must not allow your curiosity to run ahead of the narrator by asking questions: to do so would intrude into the flow of the story and break the concentration. Such an opening up of self is a preparation for what lies before your confider. The replaying of the bitter and the rueful times can throw a different light on what happened and bring forth a more objective understanding and wash away negative feelings. The story may be exposing some unconfessed and unforgiven sin of an earlier year, about which little can be done now because the one offended has died. The story may reveal years in the single state, with the loneliness and deprivation of family and children, which may at last bring the person assurance that in the future life, Jesus said that there will be neither marrying nor giving in marriage. In God's reality, eternal and unlimited love will characterize the heavenly kingdom. Whatever the nature of the revelations, happy or bitter, the relating may bring healing and comfort. Visitors should see themselves as God's instrument, bearers of God's presence to those in need. Don't force an elderly person to reveal his or her life story. Before such doors can be opened, you must have built up the older person's trust and sense of comfort in sharing some of life's deepest secrets. It may take weeks or even months to gain the privilege of hearing the elderly person's life story. Also, the person may not be in a state to face such memories of the past. This is an honor that may be accorded a sincere, genuine, caring lay visitor. Not every elderly person you visit—even over a long period—will have the need for such outpourings, but if they happen, consider it a seal of your being involved in a ministry of God's appointment for you. The person may be a very private person or have skeletons in the cupboard about which he or she is ashamed to speak. Don't despair. Your visit may be the trigger for this older person to deal with past experiences and behavior privately before God, discovering how to make peace with God. Your visit, unbeknownst to you, may have produced abundant spiritual blessings.

As a lay pastoral visitor to the aged, you are likely to be bombarded with doubts concerning God and theological issues. You need to be aware of your own faith position. Know that you depend on the Holy Spirit and not on your own abilities. Such uncertainty can weaken, or even destroy, the faith of those you visit.

People in independent living may have very sharp wits, with acute discernment, as their stage in life often makes them look for reality and find answers to their life's questions. This ministry can be most rewarding for the older person as well as for yourself as a visitor.

The Dementia Patient

Many aged people suffer from some form of dementia. Dementia involves the loss of memory,

intellect, social skills, rationality and normal social and emotional responses. Studies on dementia are somewhat inconsistent. Most suggest that
only 7 percent of those over sixty-five years develop dementia while those over eighty years
would account for 20 percent of dementia patients. Women are more prone to develop dementia, as they tend to live longer. This may help to
explain some of the increase. Thus, we may assume that 80 percent of aged people will *not* develop dementia.[6]

There are two common forms of dementia. Se-
nile Dementia of the Alzheimer's Type (SDAT)
can only be accurately verified by the autopsy of
the brain following death. The other common
type is a result of some infarction or failure of the
blood supply to the brain as in a cardiac arrest or
stroke, which causes the death of nerve cells and
tissues in the brain.

The common assumption that dementia is due
to brain disease or the deterioration of the brain
structure appears to be incorrect. Postmortem
studies of dementia cases and research in this
area show that 80 percent of moderate to severe

6. Macnab, Francis, *The 30 Vital Years* (Melbourne: Hill of Content, 1992)), 174–76.

cases of dementia do not have evidence to support that view.[7]

Some researchers, such as Kitwood in 1989,[8] suggest that the onset of dementia is most likely to be caused by social stress and other social conditions. Others suggest that it may occur slowly and be due to social and psychological changes. Loss of relationships through death, marriage breakdown, job transfers, family feuding and the loss of a home all are possible triggers of dementia. The development is slow, with increasing periods of forgetfulness, confusion and disorientation.

My own mother started to show signs of dementia at the age of seventy-four, just after my father's death. A few years later, the deterioration rapidly developed following a series of Transient Ischemic Attacks (TIA), or ministrokes. By the time she was eighty, her mind, speed and movement of limbs were almost defunct. Before she died at eighty-four, she was totally paralyzed, speechless and only responded to noises by opening her mouth to be fed like a baby bird still in the nest.

---

7. R. C. Smith et al. "Platelet Monamine Oxidase in Alzheimer's Disease," *Journal of Gerontology* 37 (1982): 572–74.

8. T. Kitwood, "Brain, Mind and Dementia: With Particular Reference to Alzheimer's Disease," *Ageing and Society* 9 (1989): 1–15.

Not all brain deterioration is due to the onset of dementia. Factors such as chronic fatigue syndrome, certain viruses, drug or alcohol abuse, dietary factors, other forms of mental illness, inadequate rest over long periods or a history of undisciplined capacity for concentration and memory control in earlier life may also contribute to dementia.

There are three stages of dementia: early, moderate, and severe. Early dementia is identified by occasional and increasing memory loss, taking longer to do simple routine tasks, difficulty in following a conversation and general vagueness.

In early dementia, a high level of anxiety may develop. Those who are affected may have seen severe dementia in others, so they embrace a dread that this is where they are heading themselves. They imagine themselves mentally incapacitated and useless. Such anxiety may accelerate the development of the dementia. This stress factor should be kept in mind when visiting a dementia patient. An elderly person with this condition needs reassurance to ease the troubled mind. This is where adequate supervised training before becoming a visitor would be advantageous.

At present, I know of one early dementia patient who is acting worse than she is to get more and more sympathy and attention. Unfortunately her husband cannot see it. At times, she slips and gives evidence of a sharp memory recall of recent happenings. Is this part of the manipulating tactic of the early dementia patient? It's difficult to tell. You need to be very wise and discerning in visiting such patients.

Moderate dementia is evidenced by short-term memory loss, while events of the distant past are recalled in great detail. Disorientation in familiar surroundings is common, along with confusion about places and times. At times, those who are afflicted with dementia may experience difficulty in remembering names and faces of family and friends. They may tend to confuse some people with others. They may become easily frustrated and angry by their deteriorating condition and uncharacteristically snap at people they love. There is a tendency to repeatedly say the same thing in the same conversation. Once fastidious about hygiene, eating and appearance, they may become sloppy and neglectful. They can become alarmed at seeing or hearing things that are not there.

Severe dementia is apparent when those afflicted need full personal care and are unable to attend to the simplest of personal needs, bringing about severe disability. When institutionalized, those who suffer from severe dementia may need to be fenced in to prevent wandering away. Many severe dementia patients wander away from the institution, causing the need for community searches.

As a pastoral visitor, remember that even though these people are disabled in many ways, they may still retain their ability to understand a conversation. So be careful about the way you speak in their presence: their feelings and emotions are still very active and can become easily hurt. Many retirement centers employ or have a regular music therapist visit the community. This therapist can help relieve agitation and encourage an inner tranquility in dementia sufferers. It is well documented that dementia patients positively respond to music and rhythm. I knew of a dying dementia patient who recognized few people—not even some family members—but who sang a few of her favorite hymns with her son as he held her hand. A week after her son told me of these experiences with her, I conducted her funeral service.

It may take time for dementia patients to show any sign of recognition of what you have said or done. But try not to appear impatient. That could cause a further blow to their dignity and self-esteem. The use of appropriate body language and touch helps keep their attention as well as convey to the dementia sufferer a sense of your presence, interest and affection.

Use short sentences with simple words. If you're trying to instill a message, do it gently and calmly, repeating the same words and using the same tone of voice. And avoid disorienting the person by reorganizing or tidying up the room. This is not your responsibility, no matter how the untidiness may irk you. Your presence, touch and gentleness alone can make the dementia sufferer's life more bearable and comfortable with her or his surroundings, so don't worry about anything else but spending some time together. For your visit to be of value, it must not be hurried.

It is possible that even people with severe dementia may understand that as a pastoral visitor, you are representing the church. Keep in mind that this simple understanding offers the opportunity of spiritual blessings for the patient.

→ THREE ←

The Nuts and Bolts of Lay Pastoral Visitation to the Aged

Church members who have a desire to visit older persons as a representative of the church must have a strong conviction that God is leading them into this ministry. To visit in the name of the church means that your words and actions are a reflection of what the church is and what it stands for. The good name of the church is affected by the way your present yourself, the way you act and the words you say. If God is directing your footsteps into this ministry, or if your church leadership has asked you to visit on their behalf, you must be constantly aware that you are also representing the Lord of the Church—Jesus Christ. In this chapter you'll find some basic guidelines for conducting your ministry.

A Word of Caution

Many people who are good talkers or have time on their hands feel they should be doing good for others. Age or family commitments may preclude employment or many other activities, or—especially if they're widowed—they may be lonely and looking for something worthwhile to fill up the hours. To these people, visiting the elderly may seem like just the ticket: after all, they may reason, older folk are just sitting, reading, watching television or just snoozing most of the day, and a visit would be a welcome diversion. These elderly people, some potential visitors may assume, just want a nice little chitchat. If that is your understanding of the aged and their needs, you should reconsider your willingness to visit in the name of the church.

Lay visitation to the elderly is more than a "do good" piece of social involvement. It is a serious commitment the church accepts on behalf of Christ, as when Christ commissioned Peter to "Feed my lambs" and "Feed my Sheep." The aged should not be considered any less than Christ's precious sheep.

Lay pastoral visitation is not a hit-and-run exercise: You call and see an aging person for the first time. You find it hard to make a conversation. They don't know you and you know little about them. They appear shy, withdrawn or just wary of someone from the church whom they don't know very well. The visit feels like a nightmare. So you just wipe that person off your visiting list as not interested. This kind of "hit and run" visitation is completely ineffectual. The only thing it accomplishes is to give the elderly person a poor opinion of the church and church people.

Those persons you failed to visit again may have been carrying a deep inner burden or grief. It is possible their hearts were aching to be poured out to someone but were uncertain in whom they could trust. Most likely, during that first visit they were assessing whether you were worthy of being trusted with their hurt. You might have relieved their lonely, tormented spirit had you shown the willingness to persist in this ministry. But by abandoning it so quickly, you've failed the elderly people you visited only once.

Preparing for Lay Ministry to the Aged

Your appointment as a lay visitor to the aged is an activity of the church community and should be undertaken with the supervision of a trained pastoral leader. You need regular access to a knowledgeable church leader.

The elderly vary in their physical, mental, social, emotional and spiritual needs. As a pastoral visitor with the minimum of training, you need someone with whom you can discuss your management of those you are visiting. Chaplains, social workers, psychologists, nurses and other professionals who are fully accredited are usually expected to be involved in in-service training and some form of case supervision. For a church lay visitor, the need is much the same. A competent person must oversee and review this ministry.

Before appointing lay pastoral visitors, a church is remiss if it doesn't provide some training in pastoral care. As a lay visitor you should have had—or be undertaking—some sort of accredited training to ensure your ministry will be fruitful and acceptable to those you visit. Such training should include instruction and practice in listening, observation and communication skills, as well as some basic orientation involving aged care.

Your Roles

Any good lay pastoral care program should be de-signed to provide helpful assistance, support and encouragement to the aged. You might be called upon to offer practical help by doing things the elderly cannot do themselves: perhaps calling a relative, running to the store to pick up a pre-scription refill, buying a new hearing aid battery or a new pair of slippers at the mall. You might need to build up emotional rapport with the eld-erly who, turning to you for advice, need to trust in your judgment. You may need to play the part of comforter in the face of an adverse diagnosis. Your pastoral care training program should pro-vide guidance for assuming all of these roles.

And as a lay pastoral visitor, your role is also a spiritual one. Over the years, the elderly people you visit have fought battles with life and possi-bly health. In their weakened resistance to pain, they may have built up a distorted view of the role God has played in certain events in their lives. In times of distress they may seek someone to blame, and God, who can't answer back and argue in person, is an obvious choice. Old age may provide ample opportunity for reflection, as the elderly seek answers to the difficult questions of their lives. The lay visitor is able to infuse some positive spiritual influence into those reflections. This perhaps is the more important function of the pastoral visitor: to whittle away at the hurdles and doubts that have impeded the flow of spiritual resources into the life of the confused, reflective older person. For many, the quest in these later years of life is to find some spiritual meaning to all that has happened over the course of a lifetime. It is a sacred privilege to help move the cataracts that blur the vision of the spiritually impaired sight of the older person.

The Prime Directives: Teamwork and Prayer

Teamwork

The important task of awakening spiritual awareness should reinforce the visitor's sense of accountability to the church. The pastoral visitor's duty is to report with a humble spirit to the group leader of the pastoral team. Such shared information enables any necessary follow-up by the church's professional staff. This may lead to reconciliation and the ministration of the sacraments. Such reporting to the group leader emphasizes the nature of the teamwork within the church's pastoral care team. Teamwork promotes fellowship, learning and bonding in ministry that invigorates the life of the church as a whole. This sense of teamwork encourages a unity of purpose within the life of the church. For a lay visitor to go off and do his or her own thing without the involvement of the wider fellowship denies the spirit that Christ sought to impregnate in the minds of his disciples. Remember when the mother of James and John came to Jesus seeking his assurance that her two sons would sit on the left and right hand of Christ in glory. The Lord will bless the humble-spirited lay visitor who willingly works within the church team.

Confidentiality

Maintaining the confidentiality of those you visit, as well as the discussions of the pastoral team, is vital to the success of the ministry. Few persons will open up to the visitor if they know that their condition and need will be publicized in the church bulletin or from the pulpit. I cringe when I hear from the pulpit or read in the church bulletin that Mrs. Jones has breast cancer and is to have surgery for the removal of her gallbladder, or that young Joe Smith has HIV. Perhaps even worse is the announcement that Charlie Doe has been admitted to the psychiatric ward with an emotional disorder that many of his family members didn't know about. Older folk mostly don't want the details of their problems broadcast to the whole community; church bulletins can end up in some strange places. Maintaining confidentiality is important for the pastoral visitor and the team to strictly observe.

That confidentiality extends to the situation that requires a referral to a skilled professional, whether it is a counselor, psychologist, psychiatrist or medical specialist. A referral shouldn't be made without the consent of the elderly person you're visiting. Also, such a referral should be made not by the lay visitor but by the senior member of the church team, in consultation with the patient and the patient's family, where possible. In dementia cases, raise any concerns you have first with the relatives.

Sometimes a lay visitor's very strong faith includes a belief in miracles and the power of prayer, whether the problem of the elderly person is physical, emotional, medical, family-related or otherwise. The ardently believing visitor, in the desire to encourage and give hope, may promise and pray for the most unbelievable miracles. Many times I have heard believing prayers for miraculous cures prove to have been ill-prayed. In such cases the patient's and the family's hopes have been so built up that when the patient dies the family loses all trust in God and in the Christian faith.

The Place of Prayer in the Pastoral Visit

Church pulpit prayers and church intercessory prayer chains almost invariably pray for healing. And it's not uncommon for charismatic evangelists to call for the sick and frail to come forth for healing. I have seen a case where a cripple threw down his crutches and started walking back to his companions, only to collapse in a heap, halfway back up the aisle, needing his crutches— an evident example of temporary psychological, psychosomatic or mind-over-matter phenomenon. When reality returned, so did the disabling condition.

In over fifty years of pastoral ministry, including eighteen years as a full-time hospital chaplain, I seldom prayed for a miraculous cure. Rather, I prayed that God, knowing the sufferer's condition, would provide the patience and strength to cope with whatever lay ahead, and that God's blessing and soothing hand would comfort with divine peace and assurance. I've prayed such prayers with hands laid, with discretion, on the affected area, and some patients have told me that they felt power surge into the area. I have seen some of my patients miraculously cured of diagnosed inoperable cancer, which still hadn't returned ten years later. I've touched the head of a twelve-year-old about to have a CT scan to determine the neurosurgeon's approach to the necessary operation, and simply said, "God bless you." The scan showed no tumor, despite previous scans clearly outlining its presence. From the moment of the blessing, that young lad did not have another headache. I did not pray for healing, yet the child was discharged 100 percent fit.

Yes! I believe in prayer and God's ability to heal. The prayer for healing must have the strong conviction of the Holy Spirit that it is God's purpose for the person. The working of the Holy Spirit is to glorify the Father and the Son in the future life of the one being prayed for. The patient must also be in tune with God for healing to take place. In the miraculous cures I have been involved in, those cured have been used by God in remarkable ministries. Their lives have been models for other Christians to observe and emulate. As the one who prayed, I cannot take any credit. It was God's doing and God must get the glory.

As a lay visitor it may be spiritually damaging to the patient and to the relatives to pray for a cure or raise unrealistic hopes during your visitations. I was abhorred one day in a hospital elevator to hear a pastoral visitor tell the mother of a young child who was terminally ill that the mother only had to pray to Jesus, who loved children, and the child would be cured. I knew the case, and knew that the child's condition was incurable and terminal. The child died a few days later.

Let me emphasize again: to raise unfulfillable expectations promising health or other miraculous outcomes can be very spiritually harmful to the family and friends of the elderly person.

In Summation

As a lay visitor to the aged, you should have a twofold purpose. By your presence you are representing the church. You are expressing the church's concern and interest in the elderly person. As an agent of the church, your every word and action will be interpreted as indicative of what the church is and what the church stands for. During your visit with the aged, there will be many observers who will be assessing and judging the church through your actions and deciding on that basis whether the church is a positive, caring institution. Every time you visit the aged, the church's reputation will be at stake. The perception of the church in the eyes of those watchers will be enhanced or downgraded by what they see. Thus, the purpose of your aged visitation should be to reflect and bring honor to the church and the God it serves.

The second purpose involves the people you are visiting and the effect your visit has on them. What will your visit impress on the mind of the older person? Does the visit confirm, assure or direct in a new way something of the apprehendable glory and compassion of God? The aim and result of your visiting is to be a greater appreciation of and acceptance of God's love in the life of the elderly people you are privileged to spend time with. Such an outcome may not be achieved in one visit but over a period of time. You won't achieve that outcome by Bible-thumping. People are more impressed by what they see than what they hear, so keep this truth in the forefront of your mind. The purpose of your visit is to radiate by your presence the tender gentleness that Jesus would display if he were in your shoes. When you enter the presence of aged persons, does a sense of peace, calm and joy coming from you begin to be felt by them? One of the greatest privileges of the visitor to the aged is to dispense the aura of God's presence into their space, wherever they happen to be.

This means that the lay visitor to the aged must continue to cultivate a close personal relationship with God, renewed daily by spiritual contemplation and communion with God before the visit is undertaken. Experience has shown that young children and the elderly are often more aware of spiritual genuineness and sincerity than people of other ages.

Lay pastoral visitation to the aged is only fruitful when there is a desire to seek and follow the Holy Spirit's guidance in the visitor's life so that the life being visited—which is also being prepared by the Holy Spirit—may experience a mutuality of fellowship with the visitor, enabling the fulfillment of God's purposes in both.

→FOUR←

Aging and Spirituality

Our mortality leaves us in no doubt that sooner or later we must die. The end result is the same for everyone, but each elderly person approaches mortality and spirituality in a different way. In this chapter, we'll take a look at the spirituality of the elderly. Consider these cases and these four ways of dealing with impending death.

Anger

Charlie, who has a variety of neuroses, has been a burden to his caregivers and his relatives. He is a nuisance and a pain in the neck as he grumbles to himself and to anybody he sees throughout the day. In this morbid state of mind, he barrages God with such questions as: "What have I done to be so old and decrepit?" "You are not fair, God—I lived a good life. Why this?" And so on, every day. Of course, he receives no audible answer from God. He sees only the grim reaper at the end of the field with his scythe and bemoans the fact that he is taking so long to get to him.

Acceptance

Susan is a lady who just turned eighty-three years old, a stalwart church member all her life who now has motor neuron disease. It is slowly creeping down her body, which has increasingly become paralyzed. Her larynx was one of the first to succumb, so she lost her speaking ability. She was given an electronic spelling board by which she fingered out her messages. Then her inability to swallow meant she had to be tube fed directly into the stomach. Her arms were the next to be paralyzed, rendering her spelling board useless and making her eyes and mouth her only means of communication, and she can use her mouth only to smile, not to talk. Despite her imprisonment within her body and confinement to her bed, she can still manage a little smile in appreciation of a visitor's presence.

Avoidance

At the age of seventy, Jessie had a coronary occlusion and was told little could be done to repair the damage to the heart. She is likely, the doctors warned, to have another cardiac arrest, or perhaps even a stroke, which could take her life, for her arteries are in so poor a condition. In other words, she has had the death sentence passed upon her. Jessie just sits in her chair most of the day, talks to no one and pretends to be asleep if anyone comes near her.

Transformation

Harold, in his midseventies, had been a serious beer drinker in his younger days. His life was so wild that by middle age he had sustained liver and kidney damage. Now in his senior years, he is confined to his bed or chair and requires dialysis three times a week. He is debilitated and uncomfortable most days and finds his restrictive life very trying. He is consoled by the fact that after his dialysis he is moved onto the verandah or into the sun in the garden, where he can enjoy the birds and watch some of the activities. Harold is grateful for the nursing home and the support the staff give him. He has a wry sense of humor, which he shares with anyone who comes near him. Some see him as the home's comic relief.

All four of these older persons have had clear warnings that the length of their days is uncertain. Before reading further, spend time considering each of these four people. Write down some of what you think may be in their minds concerning their condition and the future. Also write down what you consider to be their spiritual state and spiritual needs. As you reflect on these four cases, consider their age, their attitude to death generally, the nature of their condition, their possible spiritual status and their reactions to their imminent death. As a lay pastoral visitor, will you ignore their deepest problems by saying that you are not a theologian and that you will leave it to their minister or priest? If they continue to raise the subject of dying and the future life with you, will you feel obligated to try to deal with their questions? Remember—they are asking you because they don't want a professional coming to preach at them. You are from the church and you are a layperson. To them, you *are* the church. You should understand their position better, or so they think.

Preparation for these kinds of questions is especially important for a lay pastoral worker who visits the elderly: you should be comfortable with the thought of your own death, and with the discussion of death in general. In the death education classes that I facilitated as a chaplain, we conducted role plays in which the students faced loss and death situations. To assist some groups of students—including seminarians, government youth officers and disaster welfare workers who would be dealing with death and dying regularly—we took a visit to the city morgue, which stored up to 250 bodies and could perform sixteen autopsies at one time. It was a stark situation, but the participants needed such an experience, just in case they were called to minister in a disaster that might include multiple deaths or body mutilations. Some were initially traumatized but ultimately, after debriefing, were very appreciative of the exercise and were better able to meet death and dying situations.

A lay pastoral visitor should be comfortable and not agitated in thinking about death in general and her or his own death in particular. You need to have sorted out with God your own attitude to death before you start seriously visiting the aged. How would you react if someone told you that you had an hour to live? Facing that question is necessary if you are to have a well-rounded ministry of visitation. You will then be able to face any questions about death that the elderly may fire at you. Unless you've done this homework, you should reconsider your role as a visitor to the aged. In regular visitation to the aged, this type of issue will be hurled at you many times.

In the way they carry themselves after setbacks or traumatic events in the years prior to their senior years, you can get a glimpse into an elderly persons' spirituality, which actually has very little to do with religious affiliation and quite a lot to do with coping mechanisms.

Low Spiritual Reserves

People with low spiritual reserves are often identified by their ineffective way of coping with life's hardships. The ramifications of those events continue to be evident today. These people may also be recognized by a bitter, critical attitude to life and those around them. Nothing is ever good enough. Faults are found with everybody and everything. The chip on their shoulder is almost as big as a log. Such people have little or no spirituality, even though they may have been church members and active in the church since babyhood.

I knew of one elderly church member who was very regular in attending the Sunday service. She'd sit in the same pew each Sunday with a very sour face, never talking to anyone. When she arrived at church and saw someone else sitting in her seat, she'd turn around and go home. Did her regular attendance bolster her confidence that she was right with God? What was her motive in attending church? What did she really get out of worship? Whatever her spiritual needs were, her inapproachability made it very difficult to help her meet them. Her case is much the same as that of Charlie and Jessie. They seem to have little or no spirituality, and no vital relationship with or knowledge of God. Many like them may be seen to have a religiosity without a helpful spirituality.

Deep spiritual reserves

Susan and Harold, on the other hand, in spite of their extreme adverse physical states, nevertheless can smile and make others—including the pastoral visitor—smile and be comfortable. Staff at the retirement village also notice that these two people have many frequent visitors, both from within and outside the community.

In his younger years, Harold sowed his wild oats and partied as hard as his friends. He and his companions were far from religious: they even threw rocks on the church roof during services. To Harold and his friends, church and religion were just a big joke. But Harold's renal failure made him take stock of his life as he began to wonder whether or not there is a God. The severity of his condition made him cry out to God in prayer and he received a measure of peace. A new softness entered his spirit. Harold's newly found spirituality and discovery of a loving, caring God were bearing him along his journey during these days of suffering and infusing him with his contagious humor.

Susan found herself with one of the cruelest physical ailments. Yet because throughout her life she had sought to follow Jesus, the one she called Lord, her faith did not allow any criticism against God for her condition. The God who walked with her during her adolescent years remained with her and has stayed to the present time. The reality of her relationship with God— her spirituality—fills her with a satisfying peace.

Because her hearing is still functioning, she can replay the tapes of the weekly services and church music that the church sends her. This may be your task: to see that such an older person receives weekly tapes of inspirational messages and songs.

One particular sufferer of motor neuron disease was well-known to me. In her severely paralyzed condition not long before the end, I would mention that she would soon be reunited with her husband, who had died twelve years before, after a happy marriage of more than forty years. A smile would struggle to make an appearance and tears of joy would fill her sparkling eyes as she contemplated it. When she could finger on the spelling board, we often conversed about the Christian hope. Her anticipation of the future was eager and keen and full of joy.

Phases of Spirituality

The spirituality of persons is often gauged by their reaction to their condition during this aging period. Visitation to the likes of Susan and Harold is comparatively easy. They don't object to prayer or Scripture reading: in fact, they look forward to it. They're very happy to see a pastoral visitor and share something of their faith journey even though it may be very different from yours. You come away from such a visit elated.

In your visitation to the aged, whatever their residential situation, you must expect to come across people like these four with four different spiritual stances—and more in between. What does that say to you? The Boy Scout motto, "Be Prepared," is worth remembering. "Don't be surprised or shocked," or "Expect the unexpected," are also words to keep in your mind as you start your visitations.

Whether young or at the end of life, many people do not have any real concept of or interest in religious or spiritual matters. In the secular society of the modern era, so many consider such an interest as being for the insecure or for those who have achieved little and find in religion a place where they can draw attention to themselves or be seen as a big fish in a little pool. In many cases this is true. However this is not the whole picture.

There are three phases of religious or spiritual belief and practice:

1. *Participation in organized religious ritual practices and activities.* This is usually done

though a structured organization, with its credo of doctrines and form of rituals and worship programs.

2. *Private religious devotion, meditation or reflection.* This may follow prescribed organizational formula, or it may be developing a personal intimacy with and discovery of the divine Spirit. It may include belonging to a Christian meditation group or to another spiritual group.

3. *The outworking in daily life of the beliefs and tenets of the continuing spiritual experience.*

The first phase describes those who simply belong to a particular religious body. The majority are often nominal in their profession: their faith may have little deep-seated impact on their lives. Many of the elderly you will visit will fall into this category. Don't gauge their spiritual depth by the religious icons or Bibles that may be prominent in their living quarters. Those things may be nothing more than a talisman.

The second phase may include adherents and followers of a particular religious organization, Christian or otherwise, or they may be persons who have developed their own way of connecting with the divine, which may be no less authentic than the follower of a particular religion. Remember that God never rejects a voice that calls to him in sincerity and in truth.

The third phase is the practical development of the second. Of those persons identified with the first phase, only a minority reach this stage, where their spirituality is embodied in the way they live their life. They uphold the highest moral and ethical standards, sustained by their continuing daily personal devotions. Their faith is not so much in their words; through their lives they give evidence of the spiritual nature within them.

Susan, with her motor neuron condition, can't attend any formal worship, pick up a book and read or even write down her thoughts. Yet she was able to meditate and reflect on the God whom she worshipped. Hence the infectious uplifting radiance of her smiles, when most of her other senses were shut down.

Ministering to the Aged

In visiting the aged, you're certain to meet these three types. Chances are, you'll also meet a few nonbelievers: those who reject any divine or spiritual being and are convinced that religion is an opiate for the feebleminded.

Earlier I suggested that you expect the unexpected. Do you feel comfortable meeting with anyone from these four spiritual groups?

Regardless of who these people are and where they fit into the categories we've just looked at, each elderly person has spiritual needs that a pastoral visitor may be able to assist if the person shows the interest and desire. With your own private spiritual preparation before the visit, the accompaniment of the Holy Spirit and the prayers and support of your church fellowship, God may use you to fulfill some of those needs. Let's look at some practical ways of dealing with each of them.

The Irreligious Person

Let us take the cynical, irreligious, skeptical— even atheistic—aged persons. Their spiritual needs may be considered the greatest. Any person who is out of touch with God must be considered as having as much a priority of need as anyone else. Irreligious people have little if any idea of a life beyond the grave. For them, death might mean total annihilation. Their basic philosophy may be fatalistic: "Whatever will be, will be, and I can't do anything about it." They have little sense of guilt or accountability for sin. Although they may have a few regrets over relationships with people in the past, and some things in their lives that they might consider lost opportunities, they feel that worrying over them is useless. After all, you can't undo anything now.

When you visit them as a lay pastoral visitor, you first might only get as far as an introduction. The temptation will be to think this is unplowed territory and any seed you may drop will be eaten by the birds. But think of this: Jesus would go back because he would see a need. With such people, a sensitive compassion is required.

Your next visit may be a few sentences longer as you receive a growl to your inquiry about how this nonreligious person is feeling. This person's internal response might be, "None the better for your asking." But each time you call your visit may be a little longer until you start to hear about the person's family, earlier years and present circumstances. Over this period, perhaps you never uttered a religious phrase or offered prayer except to say "God bless you" as you left.

Perseverance is the optimum word in visiting this type of senior. Over these months you have been building trust. One day he may ask you to do something for him. It may be to pass a message to a relative or get something from the shop. A little later he may mention that he doesn't know how much longer he will be here. You might offer a simple response like, "You sound anxious about it." If you know him well enough to feel he is ready for the question, you might ask, "Are you ready for it?" This may open the opportunity for you to share your own hope for the next life. Notice that I say "share your hope." In this way, you're not telling him what to do, nor are you preaching at him, nor are you making it appear as if you are trying to convert him. You are simply sharing your experience of God. To bring out a New Testament and offer proof texts would turn the inquiry sour. It is personal belief he wants to hear about—not something secondhand that comes from a book. That, perhaps, will come later. Having shared that God has proved to be a reliable companion for you, you let the Holy Spirit water the seed that you've sown and permit the Spirit to guide you. You may even be led to say, "I'll be praying for you," as you take your leave.

Perseverance has opened the door. So far, God has guided you and will continue to do so if you are faithful. Don't be too impatient. Don't rush for a conversion or decision too quickly.

The door is open. Do let the Holy Spirit speak through you and guide you as you relate to your unbelieving senior. You are the sower. God is the reaper.

The Spiritually Alive

The sharing of ministry tapes is one of the most meaningful spiritual exercises to the older person confined to residential care, who has an active spiritual relationship with God, yet is unable to attend church services. Such residents are able to listen to the tapes or discs several times between visits. They are able to throw up points for discussion on your next visit, which turns the visit into an opportunity of most meaningful fellowship. The visitor needs to be careful not to dominate the discussion. Shut-ins need the opportunity to express their own spirituality and reflections on what they have heard during the previous week. It is possible for them to open themselves up in a way they would never have contemplated when attending church groups in earlier life. Such spiritual reverie has three implications: (1) they look forward to your regular visits and the discussions, (2) in spite of their isolation they are continuing to grow spiritually, experiencing the reality of God's presence and (3) anticipating the realization of their Christian hope in full is increasingly more exciting. Pastoral care to the aged is much more than dropping in to cheer up the elderly.

The Lukewarm Christian

What about those we might call "lukewarm" Christians or those who are merely treading water in their faith, still in the same spiritual condition that they were in forty years or more ago? They claim they believe in God (intellectually), as well as the teaching of Scripture, but there is not much more religious action in their lives than that. Spiritually they have been very complacent, particularly in their personal relationship with God himself.

Your presence as a pastoral visitor may be just the spark that stimulates their mind into considering that they should make some effort to do something about their faith just to be on the safe side for when they die. Religion, at this stage, is not seen as much more than a safety net.

They may put out some hints just to get you talking about religion. Their search may not have much substance or sincerity. Remember, they are sounding you out. It may be that they are just testing to see how genuine you are. With such people it is like tiptoeing through the tulips so as not to dampen the inquiry. Do not rush in too soon. Answer their questions and not much more for quite awhile. Avoid religious jargon, speak in simple language and avoid long explanations. Just as you would not use industrial-strength soap on a baby's skin, do not rush in with words of God's wrath, hellfire and punishment. The message of God, the message of Jesus, the message of the Holy Spirit, the message of the true Christian is the "Message of Love." Love, God's love, must be clearly expressed by your word and approach. God's love must shine strongly through the sensitive life of love they are seeing in you.

✦ FIVE ✦

Guidelines for Care

In this chapter, we'll touch upon some practical guidelines to help you provide spiritual care to the elderly you visit. And the place to begin your care, of course, is with yourself: Be sure your head is filled with an understanding of the needs of the elderly, your heart is filled with a genuine desire to help them and your soul is filled with the love of representing God before others.

Personal Preparations

Be Prepared Spiritually

A visitation on behalf of the church isn't like cooking supper. You might have watched your mother prepare meals when you were a child, or you might have watched cooking shows on television. Your culinary adventures might range from popping a frozen meal into the microwave to fixing dinner for a large family. Time and practice improve your skills.

Visitation to the aged is very different from looking after the family. Each person you visit is different because of age and health. The person may be known to you or not. One thing is certain: you can be sure that the person you are visiting today may not be as receptive as he or she was on your last visit.

I have advocated for full-time chaplains to visit each patient every day in particular units in the hospital, because there was a need for chaplains to recognize and identify changes in the patients and be able to understand their needs better. There is ample evidence that a patient's mental, emotional and medical state may vary every day. Each day demands that you must be prepared to treat the same patient differently than you did the day before. By visiting each patient daily, the chaplain is able to confront the patient's changing condition in the hospital. A pain-racked patient today will be different the next day after being given stronger painkillers. Tomorrow, who knows? They may even be less able to communicate.

Aged visitation is the same. You cannot expect to just pop in and follow a similar routine with each person you visit, or necessarily take up where you last left off. The senior you visit may have had a fall and broken a hip since you last visited. Apart from being prepared by having some training about visiting such persons, you must prepare yourself before each visit. That means spending time with your God, on whose behalf you are visiting the aged. Your own spiritual preparation is essential before you set out for a visit. Your visits may be weekly and therefore the changes may be even greater, so your task in visiting the aged may be more difficult than that of a daily visitor.

In baking a loaf of bread, you can put the dough in the oven without allowing the mixture to rise or without even adding yeast. The result will be a stodgy hunk of baked dough. By using yeast and giving it time to rise, the loaf will be light, porous, and overflow the bread tin. Similarly, your prior spiritual preparation, in a quiet place alone with God, will put the yeast into your visitation. This will make the visit palatable attractive and rewarding both for the visited and the visitor and overflowing with rich spiritual rewards.

Rely Continually on Divine Guidance during Each Visit

The one you are visiting may be experiencing changing conditions of health, distressing family or financial circumstances, the death of a friend or relative, difficulties with neighbors or relatives or other happenings that can bring joy, satisfaction, hurt or deep grief.

Your senior may not want to share any of these highs or lows with you. Her mood may be happy and relaxed, tense and agitated, open and talkative or withdrawn and tightlipped. Her acceptance of you may differ from the last visit. You may be confused by this change and uncertain about what to do. Your mind may struggle to find the words of comfort, assurance and peace your senior needs. Whatever you say seems to bring a negative response. No matter how much training or how long you've been a pastoral visitor, there will be times when you'll cry out silently within yourself, "Lord! Help me. Give me the right words to say." After decades of training and pastoral experience, there are many times when I have uttered these words, too.

Your dependence on God's help continues at every moment during your visit. Continually rely on the Holy Spirit's wisdom to help you say the most appropriate and spiritually helpful words to the one in whose presence you are in.

Acknowledge Those Words of Divine Wisdom

It's helpful to remember the nursery rhyme about Little Jack Horner. He pulled out a plum from his pudding and said, "What a good boy am I." There will be the occasions when your senior says something that backs you into a corner and leaves you at a loss for words. Then unexpectedly out of your mouth flows those plumlike words that helpfully touch the elderly person's problem or condition. Having sought the Holy Spirit's wisdom and guidance, God did not let you down. Those previously unthought of and uncharacteristic words that came out of your mouth seemed to come from nowhere. Don't say to yourself, "How clever am I," or "See how spiritual I am." Acknowledge that your helper in the visit to that person was the Holy Spirit. The words that you spoke were God's utterances, not yours. It is essential that you give God the glory and avoid spiritual pride. If pride sets in then God is unable to gift you with golden words the next time you need them.

Make Jesus Your Model

Your preparation includes steeping yourself in the way Jesus performed his ministry. Let Jesus be your role model. The word *pastoral* provides a starting point for modeling on Jesus. *Pastoral* refers to pastures and the shepherding of animals. Jesus is affectionately referred to as the "Good Shepherd." When I think of a shepherd, I think of the Himalayas, where I witnessed a shepherd leading his flock of sheep and goats, following the melting snow line to feast on the fresh, nutritious shoots of vegetation stirring after their blanket of snow had lifted. Only the best herbage was good enough for his flock. The shepherd, with the ever-watchful eye, was the companion of his animals on the journey. I heard these Himalayan shepherds call their animals by name when they strayed from the path the shepherds were leading them along. That erring sheep or goat quickly got back into line as the entire group moved up the mountain track. At night, the shepherd slept with his charges. Jesus, too, was a shepherd, guide and companion. He called his sheep—his apostles—by name: Peter, James, John, Matthew, Zacchaeus, Mary, Martha, Salome and so on. His interest in his sheep was deeply personal. He wept when Lazarus died. He was the dispenser of encouragement, enrichment, sacred words of comfort, strength and expectant hope as well as correction.

By making and modeling your visitation ministry on the Master Shepherd you are *doing* theology. Michael Taylor says, "Theology is faith expressing itself in action."[9] We need to go further. Theology is faith expressing itself in words, compassion and the tender care of others. Theology should be lived out day by day by the pastoral visitor, whose life, words and actions are motivated and activated by the model of Jesus.

Things to Avoid

Avoid Being Patronizing

Many visitors see themselves as being honored by being appointed to visit the elderly. They may see themselves as a cut above other church members. They may assess themselves as healthy and phys-

9. Michael H. Taylor, *Learning to Care: Christian Reflection on Pastoral Practice* (London: S.P.C.K., 1983), 8.

ically able compared with those who are weakened by age. Some visitors may simply consider themselves superior to the old people they visit.

Most aged persons are very conscious that their physical capabilities are lessening. For many their memory, sharpness of hearing and sight and acuteness of mind are deteriorating. Some have had their sense of dignity and their humanness shattered, never to be retrieved, and the situation will continue to worsen. To approach them with a sense of superiority and the flaunting of your faculties, and with an air of authority telling them what they should be doing or not doing, will only put them into an exaggerated tailspin.

With Jesus as your model, you will remain as a fellow human made in the image of God. Like God, be accepting and receptive of those you visit exactly as they are.

Avoid Being Manipulated

The aged have a lifetime of experiencing the world, which still operates on the premise of survival of the fittest. It is perhaps slightly different from Darwin's thesis of the primal world's struggle to survive. Many of the pre– to immediate post–World War II generation had to struggle into order to survive and maintain a modest standard of living. To do that, they may have had to deal with and overcome shrewd and competitive associates. They may have developed wiles to manipulate certain aspects of the system to gain some advantage for them. Their philosophy of life may have been to get the best out of the prevailing conditions. To do this they had to plot, scheme and use others to gain the best possible outcome of the situation for them. Many aging, whether at home or in residential care, have maintained the skills to milk the services of any of their contacts.

The church visitor is one of those whom they may perceive to be naïve enough and an easy target for manipulation. The pastoral visitor can be used as their messenger even though their other caregivers may be willing to do the errand themselves. The pastoral visitor may even be likely to fall for the not-enough-cash trick to pay for items or services, and to accept the "I'll pay you later" blurb. These elderly persons may simply expect the response of, "Don't worry about that—I'll take care of it."

Without the visitor knowing what medical or other official care instructions have been issued, the visitor can be conned into violating orders on behalf of the manipulative elderly person. I recall the case of an elderly person with renal problems who had his input and output of fluid strictly monitored. As the kidneys were not functioning as they should, any extra intake of fluid would only cause further kidney damage. He asked his visitor to get him a toothbrush and water so he could clean his teeth. The paste was put on the brush and a few brushes in the mouth were made. When the visitor gave this senior water to rinse his mouth, he grabbed the glass and swallowed the whole thing. There have been many cases when a senior has asked a visitor to go to the store and purchase a few candies or chocolates, which the senior promptly hid under the pillow. The elderly person's sugar was being carefully checked and all oral intake of food was being measured and noted for its sugar content. Such manipulation is easy to pull off with an unsuspecting, kind-hearted pastoral visitor.

A manipulative person can produce a very convincing story of unjust treatment, cantankerous fellow residents and poor quality of care. The story can be tear-jerking to get the visitor to take up the fight on the senior's behalf. Often, however, the story is an exaggeration of the events. Visitors who report these things to the pastoral care team—or even the senior's family—without further investigation may see their freedom to visit curtailed or the staff's cooperation withheld. And this incident can also affect the staff and other caregivers' attitudes toward the one who put you in that situation. Be wary.

Avoid Saying, "I know how you feel."

Pastoral visitors have kind hearts and are often affected by the sad stories of those they visit. Part of empathy is trying to imagine how another is feeling, so it's natural to spurt out the words, "I know how you are feeling." This is commonly said to hospital patients, grieving relatives and the aged. But the person to whom those words are addressed often inwardly reacts, "You liar. You cannot *possibly* know how I feel."

The reaction is true. You cannot really understand the feelings of those you visit. You have not been walking for sixty or more years in their shoes. You may have had some similar experiences, but they are not the same, nor are the circumstances. The personalities involved also may be very different. You might have had a similar surgery or medical treatment, you may have suffered the loss of a sibling or child in circumstances not altogether dissimilar to the elderly person you're visiting. But the most you can say is that you have some inkling of what they are going through because of a similar traumatic episode that you experienced in your life. There may be a likeness but the conditions are not identical. Many elderly people have told me that when they hear those words, "I know how you feel," they know the visitor cannot help them because they are too full of their own importance and just trying to impress.

The Importance of Listening

One of your most important tasks as a lay pastoral visitor to the aged is to listen deeply to whatever your seniors are telling you. Here are some tips.

Listen with Acceptance

Remember that each person's experience of life is different. Past history and circumstances are different. Even two siblings brought up in the same household can be vastly different: one can become a business tycoon while the other remains a laborer. Personalities, teachers, choice of friends, different schools, application to study, the timing of parental separation and selection of peer group may all have played a part in the difference.

Don't allow your own background and experience to dominate the way you assess the life revelations your seniors share with you. Don't allow your own experience to influence the way you appraise their character. That would be unjust and might keep you from relating compassionately as a good shepherd figure. Whatever the life history you hear, you must be accepting as Jesus accepted the woman of Samaria, the woman taken in adultery or the thief on the cross. Jesus knew their characters. Jesus shepherded men and women of all types and conditions of wholeness or sinfulness. So, too, we must accept all aging persons as children of God needing the touch of the master shepherd in their lives. As followers of Jesus, that is our commission: to accept all as they are.

Encourage the Positive Things You Hear

Toward the end of life, many aged reflect on their past. In doing so it is possible to dwell on the "might have beens" or the "if onlys" or the "I should haves." When we reminisce on the past, we can always see better options that we may have taken. A different course may have made life more enjoyable and fruitful. But dwelling on such negatives can never be helpful, nor can it change what happened. Such exercises can make anyone flounder in depression and regrets. A good shepherd's role is not to leave a member of the flock depressed. A good shepherd is able to use a highlighter on the narrative. This highlighter concentrates on positive achievements that have been helpful and productive not only personally but also for others. All of us have done many good things in our lives, which are reasons for us to be thankful to God for the strength and help he gave us to complete those good tasks.

It's the same for the aged. They might have lived a hard, tough life—even a profligate life— yet beneath the veneer of the macho or rebellious image they may have a tender side. Even former convicted criminals have positive traits that can be resurrected and dwelt upon and displayed before their minds. This helps the aging years to be lived on a positive plane, rather than allowing a reprobate past to dominate and shadow until the end. Your role is to lift your seniors out of the bog of the past and put them on a happier path.

All persons, particularly the aged, have made some helpful contributions to the lives of others, some very significant and meaningful. The size of the contributions does not matter. As a pastoral visitor to the elderly, you cannot afford to be prejudiced toward any person who has not been spiritually or even church oriented. They may have never had the opportunity to become involved. By encouraging and affirming the positives in the lives of your seniors, you can help lift their despondency and give them the same hope and acceptance they can anticipate from the forgiving God who designed them.

Encourage Mental Stimulation

To be able to listen, you need to find topics and interesting material around which a conversation can flow. For many, retirement becomes like a court sentence that puts them on death row or confines them to restricted activities. Unless they have had an active social or church life before retirement or a have family living nearby, an aging person may lose interest in life and hibernate. This is also possible if they move to a new locality. The separation from career stimulation, in many cases, brings about a collapse of interest in life generally. It is like cutting off a leg and an arm, which commences a process leading to a vegetative mental state. One of the opportunities open to a visitor of the aged is rekindling and stirring up old as well as new mind-engaging interests.

Many—those in residential care as well as those still living at home—may be found sitting comfortably in their favorite chair dozing most of the day, with little or no reason to think seriously about anything. Elderly church people may be little better: they may read only a few snippets of their Bible or short devotionals, mainly out of habit or fear of their future life if they don't.

An important opportunity to maintain the mental health of a person on your visitation list is to encourage mental stimulation. It may be advisable to make a study of what TV or radio programs or documentaries will be available over the next week. They may be highlighted for the aged person to see or hear. One or more programs may also be a focus of your conversation next visit. Encouraging your senior to think about and comment upon what she or he has seen or heard is very therapeutic.

Where the visited is an active church member or adherent, the offer of tapes of church services or other Christian teaching and music helps to encourage continuing spiritual development, as well as keeping the brain alert. Where reading is impossible, recordings of the Scriptures may be one of the most appreciated things you can offer. The church may be wise to stock several copies of such tapes.

A denominational leader who had a mastery of words was a good preacher/teacher and contributed much-appreciated articles to Christian magazines. Following eye problems that led to blindness and his admission into the nursing home, he attempted suicide. His depression was destroying him because he could not now read, write or meditate upon the Scriptures. He had numerous church leaders visit him. I urged the chaplain of his nursing home to secure a copy of the Scriptures on audio tape. His depression began to lift as he was able to listen to and meditate on the Scriptures again.

Another avenue open for the visitor is to loan Christian and other worthwhile instructive books. Novels are often mindless and mentally numbing. According to the mental ability of the person, better choices of reading material may be theological, devotional, inspirational or missionary stories. Your own bookshelves may be the source of your supply. Better still, using a church library can enhance the connection with the church as an organization. If the church doesn't have a library perhaps you can inform the church governing board of the need. Many homes contain good religious books that never come off their shelves and families may be happy to clear some space in their homes by donating the books to a church library. The library would be available to churchgoers as well as to shut-ins or others on the pastoral visitation lists.

For many seniors, reading and talking about what they have read helps to keep their minds from winding down and fossilizing. This may be an important aspect of aged visitation. Be sure to encourage mental stimulation as much as possible.

Assure Seniors of Support

There is a fine line between independence and dependence. The aging become increasingly aware of passing time. They see dependency rapidly approaching as the inroads of time weaken their physical resources and their mental alertness. The dehumanizing aspects of dependence can be a very threatening contemplation. In fact, for some it causes so much anxiety that it often hastens the degenerative process, and they fall into despondency much sooner than they should have succumbed.

The visitor to the aged, by regular visitation, can offer a ready acceptance and the encouragement to recall the positive aspects of their lives, and can hearten and boost their sense of self-worth, lifting some of the doom and gloom with which they have been filling their minds. The threat of dependency is a less bitter pill for the elderly when they have people who will sit and talk with them about the cheerful aspects of life that are still around them.

The support of lay visitors to the elderly enables a confidence that they will not have to face the future without support and encouragement. The assurance that your interest in them will continue to be available may be very important to their welfare and health. Such assurance is the tonic they need to cope with the slowing of their ability to battle with their advancing years. Your ministry as a church lay visitor adds another dimension, in that it provides the knowledge that they have the support of the church and the God the church serves.

Avoid Overzealousness

One of the quickest ways to put an end to pastoral visits is to be overzealous. People who are advancing in years think and do things more slowly. They cannot be rushed.

As a church visitor you've learned that your spiritual ministry is to visit the aged. You've been told—directly or indirectly—that you're a missionary and the aged are your mission field. There is a further connotation: a missionary's task is to lead people to make a decision for Christ. Some visitors use this concept as mandate to accomplish this end in the shortest possible time, as there may never be another opportunity.

A zealous missionary visitor who calls on the elderly with this "now-or-never" mentality will have a short-lived ministry to the aged. Without first listening to and understanding the stories that seniors have to tell, your efforts to haul out the Scriptures and turn the screws to extract a confession, witness repentance and claim a conversion could go horribly wrong. Your efforts could turn into spiritual murder by driving your seniors further from God and the church.

Such pressurized evangelism is usually rejected, with righteous resentment and rage. This type of overzealousness also harms the Kingdom of God, as not only the aged but their relatives and other visitors are angered as they learn what happened. Evangelical approaches must be raised only after close listening to your seniors. Before you can offer Christ to them, you need to know something about their spiritual condition and their readiness for such an encounter.

God's timing is the best timing. An evangelical intrusion into the visit should only be made where there is clear and strong evidence that the Holy Spirit has been working in the mind and heart of the person you are visiting. There are usually telltale signs or leads showing you where and when not to raise the issue of an eternal future. In visitation, I've been amazed as to how and when God opens the door. God never makes mistakes but we humans certainly do. In raising evangelical issues with the elderly, be wary that you are not making a mistake.

Avoid Anecdotal Stories

As your seniors tell their stories, you may start to recall similar experiences of your own. It's easy to get excited and want to tell your account. But doing this can be an intrusion that distracts you from listening to what seniors are saying. They are telling about certain experiences in *their* life, and it's important for them to finish what they're saying. You may be able to top it with what you or someone else lived through or experienced in somewhat similar circumstances. But visitation can be turned into a game of "one-upmanship" or "whatever you can relate I can relate one better."' That is not visitation.

If you butt in with a more gruesome or more painful anecdote, you may fill your senior with a greater dread and fear, causing increasing mental and physical problems. If you do share an anecdote from your own life, make sure it has a positive outcome that doesn't leave the elderly persons further distressed, with a souring outlook about the state of their health and their future.

Beware, too, of telling anecdotes that break a confidence or cast aspersions on another person your hearer—or hearers—may know.

Avoid Medical Pronouncements

We all come across people who are aging or have one or other serious physical or mental illnesses. When your elderly person tells a story of a particular medical condition such as cancer, cardiac failure, a psychiatric issue, or another serious condition, you may be tempted to tell of the outcome of another person who had the same complaint.

As children, just about all of us had a neighbor who loved to gossip and talk over the fence. She would read the newspaper from front to back, and then watch out for the first person she saw to inject her or him with all the morning's reports of people who had been involved in some gruesome event or had some illness with dire consequences. Hardly a day passed without the quip after such a session, "My sister Jinny had that and she died." Over the years, sister Jinny must have had every complaint in the book.

Try not to be like that gossipy neighbor. To pass on to an aged person the medical outcomes of people with certain medical conditions is one of the big "no-nos" of pastoral visitation. When you listen to your senior's report, make no comparison with any other situation. You do not know the full medical condition of the person you're visiting, nor can you be fully aware of all the circumstances of the other case unless you're a fully qualified medical practitioner; even then you'd probably be assuming some factors. It's most probable that there are things about the condition and the treatment that you're not aware of or simply don't understand.

Remember that people's bodies do not react or respond to a disease or its treatment in the same way. At times, doctors can disagree over a diagnosis and treatment of the same patient. I've sat in on too many Hematology Unit weekly clinical meetings to not be aware that serious illnesses, in spite of scans and other tests, can leave doctors in several minds. Some doctors prefer one method of treatment; others may opt for a different one altogether. The chemotherapy protocol for a patient would be changed according to the patient's response, and the pros and cons for change were sometimes hotly debated until a consensus was reached. So how can you—as a lay visitor—make comparisons between people with similar symptoms? It's a dangerous practice to engage in such discussions with the elderly person you're visiting. Should it so happen that your grim comparison was right, then you may have put unnecessary psychological pressure on the patient too soon. In other words, you could have scared them to an earlier death. If you're wrong and gave unwise hope, then your senior's trust in you may have been irreparably damaged. You are a church visitor. Your job is to listen and care, and not to be a soothsayer.

Understand the Hidden Message of Your Senior's Story

"Why the fear?" you may wonder. If your seniors give a clear indication that they're apprehensive about what's likely to happen to them, you must listen very carefully. What is the root of this fear? In some cases they have seen parents or other associates endure painful and long drawn-out periods of anxiety before their deaths. Others in a similar situation are more concerned about reviewing and contemplating their life from childhood to the present.

Such reviewers may become agitated and fearful by their churning over many of their earlier deeds and actions. Any life—especially a long one—contains memories both good and bad. And now, near the ends of their lives, elderly people may keep regurgitating some of those occasions when they hurt other people and their interests. It is impossible to reverse those effects. Thoughts go on in their mind like, "Is God now punishing me for those things that I did?" "Can God forgive me?" "I'm not a fit person to meet God" or "I'm heading for hell."

Some troublesome, anxiety-producing thoughts may carry more than an undertone of guilt. It is a guilt that ulcerates the mind, disturbs sleep patterns and requires the administration of sedative drugs. This fear may be directly due to unforgiven sin, which may appear to elderly people to be alienating them from God at this critical time. This is God probably opening the door for you to create an awareness of God's ability to forgive them, if they will forgive themselves and others who may have hurt them. If possible, they should forgive others who have harmed them in earlier days. Explain how God cannot forgive unless they are prepared to forgive, as the Lord's Prayer says. If the person they have harmed is still alive, help seniors to make the contact by telephone or mail. If contact is impossible, gently encourage your senior to leave the matter in the hands of God, as they confess their wrongdoing to God and seek God's forgiveness.

Don't pressure the elderly to make the confession before you. They may be too ashamed and embarrassed over what they did. It may be too personal. Such insistence may squash any further responsiveness to your ministry. An alternative may be to offer to contact their minister, priest or some other Christian whom they know and trust. Should they be of another religion, then perhaps summon their imam, priest, or lama. Remember, you are only God's servant. It is only God who can forgive and offer eternal life.

Listen for Flaws in the Stories of the Elderly

Remember that the persons you are visiting may not have the same mental acumen and clarity of thinking they once enjoyed. They may be preoccupied with things happening within their own life and in the lives of their families. Their constant dwelling on such things tends to distort the actual situation. Many aging people tend to make mountains out of molehills.

What you hear may be an exaggeration of the facts. You may need to sit quietly with the elderly as they tell you what happened. This may be an opportunity to tease out the facts and put them into some perspective. In such cases, the evidence may show that things weren't nearly as bad as they were reported to you or as they feared they might be. Such sorting out often relieves much unnecessary stress and helps seniors to put the matter behind them. Don't be surprised if you need to return to the same ground several times, since the visited may require further reassurance before it really sinks in.

As a pastoral visitor, you must be aware of flaws and exaggeration in some of the stories you may hear. Take into consideration the senior's amount of mental deterioration. If your senior is in residential care or being cared for within the family, responding to accusations or reacting too quickly to complaints against family or staff—without sufficient tactful inquiry—can cause a lot of unnecessary angst.

Listen to your seniors' stories and *hasten slowly* to react. Let me stress once more: Endeavor to direct the attention of the elderly to positive and happy times. In their state of mind, it may be easier to do than you think. Direction to past or present happy times can often dispel many perceived aggravations.

The Reflective Review

Perhaps one of the weakest aspects of lay visitation is that once the visit is over, visitors give it little serious thought until the next visit or the minister's or priest's inquires about how the ministry is going. It's important to find a quiet place after every day's visitation and reflect on what transpired between you and those you visited.

Write down the name and set down your estimation of the mental, physical and spiritual state of the elderly persons you visited. On the basis of that assessment, consider what you remember of the conversation and what particular items dominated. Did their emotional mood alter with a change of subject? If so, why did you think that change happened? Was there something in the change that you picked up or failed to pick up? Did you say something that provoked agitation or calm? Did that emotional shift indicate any previously unrecognized anxiety, or was it an indication that a few topics especially animate them? It's important to note these things and to use such knowledge for future visits. Was there a subject they skirted around and didn't want to talk about? Was there an avoidance of any spiritual conversation? Why do you think so? In your review, consider whether you won more or less confidence and trust in yourself as a result of the visit.

A careful analysis of the visit should help you become aware of differences, of opportunities for spiritual care and of matters that could be the focus of your next visit, if you can introduce them without making your senior uncomfortable. As always, you must not force your agenda but let matters arise naturally. Be quick to note any positive or negative reactions if those matters do arise. Carefully consider your analysis when you make your own spiritual preparation before your next visit. Keep these topics in mind as you seek prayerful spiritual guidance.

Visitation to the aged is essentially a ministry of the church to the aged. It is not a ministry of just breezing in and out, but a serious piece of Christian service. All such tasks of the church in Christ's name should be undertaken in all seriousness with the offering of only the best effort you can make.

Paul wrote in 2 Timothy 2:15: "Do your best to present yourself to God as one approved by him, a worker who has no need to be ashamed. . . ." May the words of the Greatest Shepherd crown your efforts on your triumphant entry into the Kingdom of Heaven: "Well done, good and trustworthy slave; you have been trustworthy in a few things, I will put you in charge of many things; enter into the joy of your master" (Matthew 25:21).

What Is Pastoral Care for the Aged?

Care is one of the basic human instincts toward others. This is mutual between normal people, each giving and receiving care from the other. Care becomes evident through helpful acts and words of support or counsel.

Care becomes pastoral when it reaches beyond the human context to share the care that the eternal source of human life offers the entire world.

Pastoral care to the aged also endeavors, through relationships expressed in words, acts and empathetic understanding, to share the reality of God's presence and love to those coming toward the end of their earthly life. For the aged, pastoral care has greater significance as it can provide the opportunity to listen to eternal truths in preparation for entry into the unfamiliar and the unknown future life.

Your task is to offer this care without causing antagonism by unwanted intrusion into the elderly person's privacy. Keep your listening and observation skills sharp!

→APPENDIX 2←

The Pastoral Art of Listening

Pastoral listening has a different style from the way a counselor, a doctor, a therapist or a spiritual director listens to a patient or a client.

The ultimate purpose of pastoral listening is to bring the gentle touch of the Master Shepherd into the conscious realm of the person being visited. The elderly person is nearing the end of life's journey with, perhaps, many long-buried inner concerns now becoming relevant. Pastoral visitors to the aged must have three essentials:

1. *The ability to listen to and understand their own inner self and the commitment to the regular practice of self-listening.* Unless pastoral visitors are able to understand their own inner selves, they cannot set aside their own per-

sonal prejudices, views and indoctrinations on life to clearly listen to another. This ability can keep visitors from becoming inappropriately emotionally involved with those they visit. Lack of it can leave visitors open to manipulation, inefficiency and burnout.

2. *The motivation to care for and to listen to the aged.* If the motivation is right, concentration on listening isn't sidetracked by personal agendas, leaving the aged comfortable enough to respond openly to the visitor.

3. *The humility to recognize that they are not professionals.* When pastoral visitors understand their own inner self and have the right motivation for their ministry, they're more readily able to recognize what is best for their seniors and more ready to a make a referral to a qualified person. When getting out of their depth, visitors should not hesitate to recognize their own limitations.

The older person must have the confidence that the visitor is a good listener. There are several factors that make acceptance possible:

- Eye contact expresses interest and attention.
- Sit relaxed, alert but not limp, casual or tense.

- Face the person directly.
- Have an open stance: do not fold your arms, present your side to the person or sit slouched.
- Try not to sit too close to avoid seeming threatening or intimidating.
- Leaning slightly forward and not back shows your interest and engagement.
- Respond to the speaker with appropriate body movements.
- Show genuine concentration on what is being said.
- Do not fiddle with objects such as a pencil, keys and so on. Don't drum your fingers as your seniors are speaking—that shows lack of interest or an air of impatience.
- Note the speaker's body language for any signs of discomfort, tiredness or agitation (see appendix 3).

Nonverbal Communication Indicators

In many cases communication between individuals involves words that carry less influence than bodily movements and expressions. Nonverbal signals are communicated by each person in any encounter. In visiting the hospital patient, irrespective of role, the visitor needs to observe these telltale pointers to understand the message that the patient, relative or staff is really sending. Outlined here are some of these message-carrying signs that you should observe at the bedside.

Both during and after visits, try to recall those indicators. Remember that *you also* relay messages with your own voice and body. At the time of each visit, be aware of the countermessages you may be signaling. Assess how you think the patient is reading you.

Facial expressions and appearance

POSITIVE	NEGATIVE
Warm, inviting, smiling	Cold, stiff, distant
Appropriate dress	Too formal, too casual dress
Groomed appearance (hair, makeup)	Careless appearance
Good eye contact	Roving or staring eyes, or no direct contact

Voice modulation

POSITIVE	NEGATIVE
Warm, natural	Dull, monotone
Circumspect tone	Embarrassingly loud or too soft
Understandable rate of speech	Too fast or too clipped speech
Fluent language	Stuck for words
Empathetic (understanding, supporting tone)	Artificial, false, insincere
Audible responses (*hm, hmm, aha,* etc.)	Hesitant, with many *ers, ums, ahs*
Appropriate silent gaps (for reflection)	Embarrassed silence with fidgeting
Interrupting to clarify or reflect before proceeding	Saying "yes, yes" when it should be "no"

Body posture

POSITIVE	NEGATIVE
Leaning toward person at eye level	Sitting side on (discouraging to relationship and interaction)
Comfortable and relaxed position, settled, making it obvious that time is no problem	Cold, rigid, impersonal attitude; remaining standing and authoritative in position; looking ready to leave momentarily
Where possible, being three to four feet distant	Too distant or too close

Gestures and manners

POSITIVE	NEGATIVE
Extended, accepting arm/s	Arms by the side, in an indifferent manner
Firm handshake if appropriate	Limp handshake
Keeping head and body turned toward patient to indicate full attention; making patient the center of conversation	Talking to others, ignoring patient, yawning, fidgeting with anything, looking frequently at clock or watch

The Church and
Lay Pastoral Ministry

A century ago and earlier, people around the
world were identified by their extended family
and their religious affiliation. A religious alle-
giance was the principle formula for a society's
structure and loyalty. A hierarchical priestly system denoted society's pecking order. In more
primitive cultures, even the tribal chief consulted
the animist priest, soothsayer or medicine man
who had the powers of authority. A person with
epilepsy was considered to be in touch with the
spirit world and therefore was a respected priest
or diviner of spiritual causes and outcomes. Even
in premodern Christian communities, the church
and its priest were the hub and influential power
in the lives of the villagers.

Over the last century the power of the church and the fear of clergy authority have all but dissipated. Societies in the humanistic technological era with their emphases on democracy and the rights of the people have increasingly relegated the authority of the church and religion to a secondary role. This has also led to a breakdown of the influence of the extended family, respect for elders and their teaching and a cynical attitude toward the moral, spiritual and ethical ethos for which the church stands.

Many of the life situations faced by individuals and the community are not mended by legislation or secular or community authorities. Many of the social problems faced by the populace are spiritual and may be helped by spiritual intervention. More and more people are floundering and sinking deeper and deeper into depression and despair. In many cases, sedative and psychiatric medications are able to assist but unable to cure the condition. The source of the problem has to be dealt with. Today, the church's task is to go into the community and care for such people in needy situations, and this is much more demanding and urgent than in any previous time. Secular therapists are in demand in many cases that by rights should be picked up and covered by the church's pastoral care program before the degeneration of patients requires such professional help.

Within its membership, the church has people who are trained and skilled enough to equip and send out carers to offer pastoral assistance to the desperate.

The church's role is to:

- Select suitable people
- Train those selected
- Supervise and support its team

To Select Suitable People

In Ephesians 4, Paul talks about the unity within the church and how God calls and appoints certain people to specialized ministries within the church, including pastors. Not all are called to be pastors or pastoral visitors to the people who have spiritual and other needs. From Paul's chapter, we can gather that pastoral function is an important task of the church. The church, in the earlier part of the last century and before, saw the priest or minister as the pastor or shepherd of the flock. If anyone was in need then the pastor was called to attend to the person. I recall an elderly woman who demanded a pastoral call every week. It had to be the senior minister. The assistant minister's visits were not considered pastoral.

However, following World War II, the idea of lay pastoral care has been increasingly advocated, practiced and accepted. It has since become the responsibility of the church to select, appoint and train such pastoral workers and visitors who go out in the name of the church. Some who gossip or are often nosy are the first to volunteer as pastoral visitors with or without church sanction, and they can do much harm.

What type of persons should the church seek out and train to be pastoral visitors? Let us list some of the characteristics. They should:

- have a deep spiritual experience
- have a spiritual awareness of others' needs
- have a personality that is inviting, open, warm and friendly
- have an approachability that is quickly able to reassure and build confidence
- be able to encourage responsive dialogue
- show evidence that they understand the situation
- be accepting and nonjudgmental of the person

- be sensitive enough to be aware of underlying and unspoken problems
- be tactful and know what to say and when and when not to say it
- be ready to pick up positives and promote them
- have an empathy that helps the person to prioritize needs and deal with the more pressing ones first (this may mean dealing with material concerns before relational and spiritual problems, with the aid of the pastoral visitor)
- be flexible and change opinions and courses of action as further insights into the situation are gleaned
- preserve personal integrity by always acting discretely, keeping promises and maintaining confidentiality
- utilize listening skills that are essential to retain interpersonal trust and confidence
- readily recognize the nature of emotional, practical and spiritual support the person requires

Train Those Selected

It would be unheard of to appoint a teacher to a school without some classroom training. So it is unwise to let a pastoral visitor loose upon needy people whether it be in a hospital, retirement village or their own home without adequate pastoral training. It is equally essential and important that pastoral care visitors should have some training that conforms to some recognized standard. Poor pastoral care can psychologically and spiritually further complicate the lives of the persons visited.

The church can facilitate such training by appointing and establishing a pastoral care team. This team may be involved in the selection of the pastoral visitors, according to the church's criteria, and they will be responsible for the determination of each person's training program. Pastoral care training courses organized by reputable Christian organizations for this purpose may be utilized. The church may have qualified persons it can call upon to run its own training courses. Some tertiary institutions have pastoral care courses that issue accredited certification.

To Supervise and Support Team Members

Efficient chaplaincy teams in hospitals meet at least once a month for in-service training and supervision, often presented by team members or other specialists. The chaplains also present their work, which is then discussed and evaluated by peers, with problems and suggestions aired publicly. At other times, chaplains may talk over difficult cases with other chaplains for advice, correction and encouragement.

If pastoral visitors need such training and supervision, then they require similar support to make them more skillful and efficient in their ministry. Some churches organize their pastoral care team to meet monthly. I have been invited to a number of different churches to provide input for their monthly support and supervisory sessions. In these sessions a strong bond of trust, cooperation and fellowship is evident. There is a liberty for visitors to voice their concerns about their work or a particular case, or to seek some debriefing after a particularly traumatic case.

These churches' teams are very successful, building up a high reputation for the church in the community. Through the caring love of trained pastoral visitors from the church many have gained entry into the kingdom of god and into the supportive fellowship of the church.

www.ingramcontent.com/pod-product-compliance
Lightning Source LLC
Jackson TN
JSHW081318130125
77033JS00011B/344

* 9 7 8 0 8 1 9 2 2 2 1 3 8 *